To the Reader . . .

The books in this series include Hispanics from the United States, Spain, and Latin America, as well as from other countries. Just as your parents and teachers play an important role in your life today, the people in these books have been important in shaping the world in which you live today. Many of these Hispanics lived long ago and far away. They discovered new lands, built settlements, fought for freedom, made laws, wrote books, and produced great works of art. All of these contributions were a part of the development of the United States and its rich and varied cultural heritage.

These Hispanics had one thing in common. They had goals, and they did whatever was necessary to achieve those goals, often against great odds. What we see in these people are dedicated, energetic men and women who had the ability to change the world to make it a better place. They can be your role models. Enjoy these books and learn from their examples.

Frank de Varona
General Consulting Editor

General Consulting Editor
Frank de Varona
Associate Superintendent
Bureau of Education
Dade County, Florida, Public Schools

Consultant and Translator
Alma Flor Ada
Professor of Education
University of San Francisco

Editorial
Barbara J. Behm, Project Editor
Judith Smart, Editor-in-Chief

Art/Production
Suzanne Beck, Art Director
Kathleen A. Hartnett, Designer
Carole Kramer, Designer
Eileen Rickey, Typesetter
Andrew Rupniewski, Production Manager

Copyright © 1993 Steck-Vaughn Company

Library of Congress number: 89-38017

Library of Congress Cataloging in Publication Data

Gleiter, Jan
    Benito Juárez.
    (Raintree Hispanic stories)
    English and Spanish.
    Summary: A biography of the Mexican president who during his tenure in office separated church and state, established religious tolerance, and made the land distribution system more equitable.
    1. Juárez, Benito, 1806–1872—Juvenile literature. 2. Mexico—History—1821–1872—Juvenile literature. 3. Presidents—Mexico—Biography—Juvenile literature. [1. Juárez, Benito, 1806–1872. 2. Mexico—History—1821–1872. 3. Presidents—Mexico.] I. Title. II. Series.
F1233.J9G57 1989 972'.07'092 [B] [92]   89-38017

ISBN 0-8114-8476-8 hardcover library binding

ISBN 0-8114-6759-7 softcover binding

    5 6 7 8 9 0 97 96 95

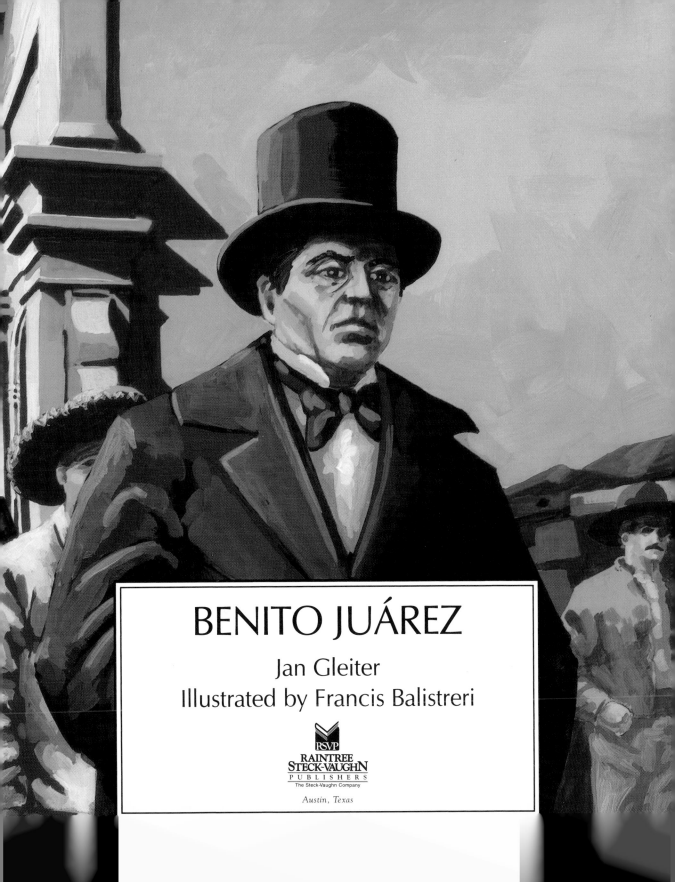

BENITO JUÁREZ

Jan Gleiter
Illustrated by Francis Balistreri

RSVP
RAINTREE
STECK-VAUGHN
PUBLISHERS
The Steck-Vaughn Company

Austin, Texas

High up in the mountains, in the state of Oaxaca in Mexico, there is a village called San Pablo Guelatao. There, in a two-room house with a dirt floor, Benito Juárez was born on March 21, 1806.

Benito's parents were Zapotec Indians, and they were very poor. When Benito was three years old, both of his parents died. Benito and his two older sisters went to live with his grandparents, who died a few years later. Benito was then sent to live with his uncle, Bernardino Juárez. Benito's uncle wanted him to be educated, but there was no school in the village.

Benito's uncle tried to teach Benito what he knew, but there was not much time for lessons. Most of Benito's time was spent working in the fields, farming and herding sheep.

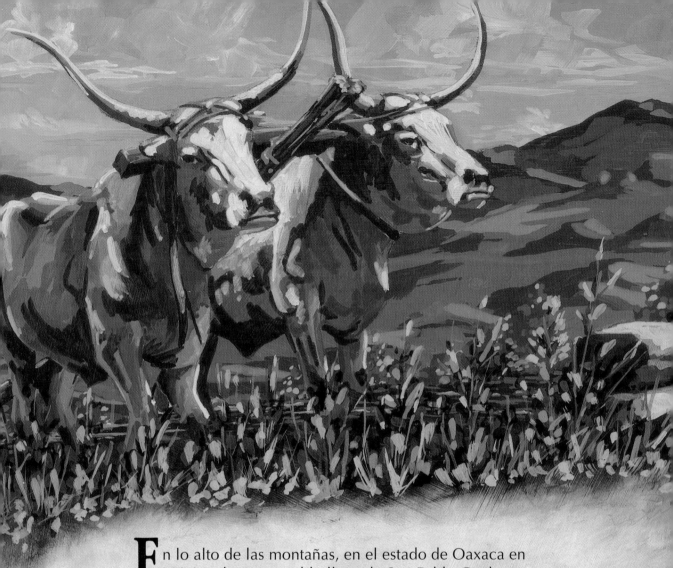

En lo alto de las montañas, en el estado de Oaxaca en México, hay un pueblo llamado San Pablo Guelatao. Allí, en una casita de dos cuartos, con piso de tierra, nació el 21 de marzo de 1806, Benito Juárez.

Los padres de Benito eran indios zapotecas y eran muy pobres. Cuando Benito tenía tres años, murieron su padre y su madre. Benito y sus dos hermanas mayores fueron a vivir con sus abuelos, que murieron pocos años después. Benito fue enviado a vivir con su tío, Bernardino Juárez. Su tío quería que Benito se educara, pero en el pueblo no había escuela.

El tío de Benito trató de enseñarle todo lo que él sabía, pero no había mucho tiempo libre para el estudio. Benito se pasaba la mayor parte del tiempo trabajando en los campos, sembrando y pastoreando las ovejas.

Benito knew that the only way he could learn the things he wanted to know was to go to the city. One day, when he was twelve years old, he ran away from his small mountain village and walked forty miles to the city of Oaxaca. He found the house where one of his sisters worked as a cook. The family she worked for, the Mazas, were kind to the thin, ragged little boy. He stayed with them until they found him a job working in the home of a bookbinder. This man was also kind to Benito and sent him to school, but the education he received was a poor one.

Benito sabía que irse a la ciudad sería el único modo de aprender todo lo que quería. Un día, cuando tenía doce años, se fue sin permiso del pueblecito de las montañas y caminó cuarenta millas hasta la ciudad de Oaxaca. Encontró la casa en la que una de sus hermanas trabajaba de cocinera. La familia para la cual trabajaba, los Maza, fueron bondadosos con el chiquillo delgado y andrajoso. Se quedó con ellos hasta que le consiguieron trabajo en la casa de un encuadernador de libros. Este hombre también fue bondadoso con Benito y lo mandó a la escuela, pero la instrucción que recibió fue muy pobre.

It was not easy to be an Indian in a country where people of Spanish blood had all the advantages. Even at school, the Indian children were mostly ignored. It was difficult for Benito to get the education he wanted so badly, but he went from one school to another and learned what he could.

When he was twenty-two, Benito Juárez entered the Institute of Arts and Sciences and studied many things, including law. When he was twenty-five, he finished school and began work as a lawyer. In 1834, he passed the exams that allowed him to argue cases in the highest courts.

No era fácil ser indio en un país en que la gente de descendencia española tenía todas las ventajas. Aun en la escuela los niños indios recibían poca atención. Era difícil para Benito obtener la instrucción que tanto deseaba, pero fue de escuela en escuela y aprendió todo lo que podía.

Cuando tenía veintidós años, Benito Juárez ingresó al Instituto de Artes y Ciencias y estudió muchas cosas, incluso derecho. Cuando tenía veinticinco años, completó sus estudios y empezó a trabajar de abogado. En 1834 aprobó los exámenes que le permitieron defender casos en las cortes de más importancia.

While Juárez was working as a lawyer, he frequently defended poor people who were accused of crimes. He usually did not charge these people for his work. In 1841, he became a judge. The idea of justice, of being fair, was extremely important to Juárez. That, combined with his intelligence, honesty, and patience, made him a good judge.

Through the years, Juárez had remained friends with the Maza family. When he was thirty-seven, he married Margarita Maza, who was only seventeen. Even though there were twenty years between their ages, Benito and Margarita Juárez were devoted to each other. They had twelve children.

Mientras Juárez trabajaba de abogado, defendía a menudo a la gente pobre que había sido acusada de algún delito. Casi nunca les cobraba por sus servicios. En 1841 pasó a ser juez. La idea de la justicia, de ser justo, era extremadamente importante para Juárez. Por eso y por su inteligencia, su honradez y su paciencia, fue un magnífico juez.

Juárez había seguido siendo amigo de la familia Maza a través de los años. Cuando tenía treinta y siete años, se casó con Margarita Maza, que tenía sólo diecisiete años. A pesar de que había veinte años de diferencia entre ellos, Benito Juárez y Margarita Maza de Juárez se querían mucho. Tuvieron doce hijos.

The government of Mexico had been in a state of constant change since 1821. In that year, Mexico had won independence from Spain. However, Mexico did not have a strong government to replace the Spanish one. Power seesawed back and forth between the two main political parties. When power changed hands, the change was not usually peaceful. Many people died in the fighting and the riots.

The two political parties were the Conservatives and the Liberals. The Conservative party supported the Roman Catholic church and wanted wealthy landowners to rule the country. The Liberals were in favor of free elections and wanted to improve the conditions of the poor. They thought that the Roman Catholic church had too much power.

El gobierno de México había sufrido cambios constantes desde 1821. En ese año se había logrado independizar de España. México, sin embargo, no tenía un gobierno fuerte para reemplazar al español. El poder pasaba de uno al otro de los dos partidos políticos principales. Cuando el poder cambiaba de manos no era usualmente en forma pacífica. Mucha gente murió en las luchas y revueltas.

Los dos partidos políticos eran los conservadores y los liberales. El Partido Conservador apoyaba a la iglesia Católica Romana y quería que los ricos terratenientes gobernaran el país. Los liberales estaban a favor de las elecciones libres y querían mejorar las condiciones de vida de los pobres. Pensaban que la iglesia Católica Romana tenía demasiado poder.

13

The Roman Catholic church was very different then. Priests charged money to baptize people, to hear confessions, and to do their other jobs. The church controlled the banks, owned mines and huge amounts of land, and had more money than the Mexican government. However, it paid no taxes. If a priest or other employee of the church was accused of a crime, he or she was not tried in a regular Mexican court but in a church court. The church did not want any changes in Mexican life. It had an enormous amount of power and wanted to keep it.

Juárez was a Roman Catholic, but he was also a Liberal. He was willing to fight for justice, even if he had to fight against the church.

La iglesia Católica Romana era muy distinta entonces a lo que es hoy en día. Los sacerdotes cobraban dinero por bautizar a las personas, por oír confesiones y por prestar sus otros servicios. La iglesia controlaba los bancos, era dueña de minas y de grandes extensiones de tierra y tenía más dinero que el gobierno de México. Sin embargo, no pagaba impuestos. Si un sacerdote u otro miembro de la iglesia era acusado de un delito, no se le juzgaba en los tribunales mexicanos sino en un tribunal de la iglesia. La iglesia no quería que hubiera ningún cambio en la vida mexicana. Tenía un enorme poder y quería conservarlo.

Juárez era católico, pero era también liberal. Estaba dispuesto a luchar por la justicia, aun si eso implicaba luchar contra la iglesia.

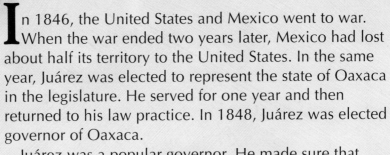

In 1846, the United States and Mexico went to war. When the war ended two years later, Mexico had lost about half its territory to the United States. In the same year, Juárez was elected to represent the state of Oaxaca in the legislature. He served for one year and then returned to his law practice. In 1848, Juárez was elected governor of Oaxaca.

Juárez was a popular governor. He made sure that people paid their taxes. He used the money to build clinics, hospitals, schools, roads, and bridges. He remembered how difficult it had been for him, as a poor Indian, to get an education. Therefore, he made sure that the new schools in Oaxaca welcomed Indian students—both boys and girls. When his term as governor was over, Juárez returned to his law practice.

En 1846, hubo una guerra entre los Estados Unidos y México. Al terminar la guerra, dos años después, México había perdido más o menos la mitad de su territorio, que había pasado a ser de los Estados Unidos. Ese mismo año, Juárez fue elegido para representar al estado de Oaxaca en la legislatura. Ejerció por un año y luego regresó a ejercer de abogado. En 1848, Juárez fue elegido gobernador de Oaxaca.

Juárez gozó de popularidad como gobernador. Se aseguró de que la gente pagara los impuestos. Usó el dinero recaudado para construir clínicas, hospitales, escuelas, caminos y puentes. Se acordaba qué difícil había sido para él, un indio pobre, obtener instrucción. Por eso se aseguró que las nuevas escuelas de Oaxaca trataran bien a los alumnos indios, tanto los niños como las niñas. Cuando su período como gobernador terminó, Juárez regresó a ejercer derecho.

In 1853, the president of Mexico was Antonio López de Santa Anna. He was a Conservative who hated all Liberals and especially Benito Juárez. One day, while Juárez was working, he was arrested. He had committed no crime, but people who disagreed with the government were often in great danger. Juárez was kept in jail for several months and was then put on a ship bound for Europe. The English captain disapproved of what had been done to Juárez and let him go ashore in Cuba. From there, Juárez made his way to New Orleans, Louisiana, in the United States.

En 1853, el presidente de México era Antonio López de Santa Anna. Era un conservador que odiaba a los liberales y en particular a Benito Juárez. Un día, a Juárez lo arrestaron mientras trabajaba. No había cometido delito alguno, pero las personas que no estaban de acuerdo con el gobierno estaban a menudo en gran peligro. A Juárez lo retuvieron en la cárcel por varios meses y luego lo embarcaron en un barco que iba a Europa. El capitán del barco, que era inglés, no estaba de acuerdo con lo que le habían hecho a Juárez y lo dejó desembarcar en Cuba. Desde allí Juárez pudo llegar a Nueva Orleáns, en Luisiana, en los Estados Unidos.

In New Orleans, Juárez worked with other Mexican Liberals on plans to overthrow Santa Anna. In Mexico, that struggle was being led by Juan Álvarez. After two years, Juárez sneaked back into Mexico and joined the revolution. In 1855, the Liberals took control of the government. Álvarez became the president. He named Juárez as the minister of justice.

Juárez persuaded the legislature to pass one of the most important laws in the Mexican reform movement. It was called the Juárez Law, and it did away with separate courts for the church and the army. For the first time, all Mexicans were equal under the law. Another reform forced the church to sell much of its property. Most important, in 1857, the reform movement created a constitution. The constitution took away much of the church's power.

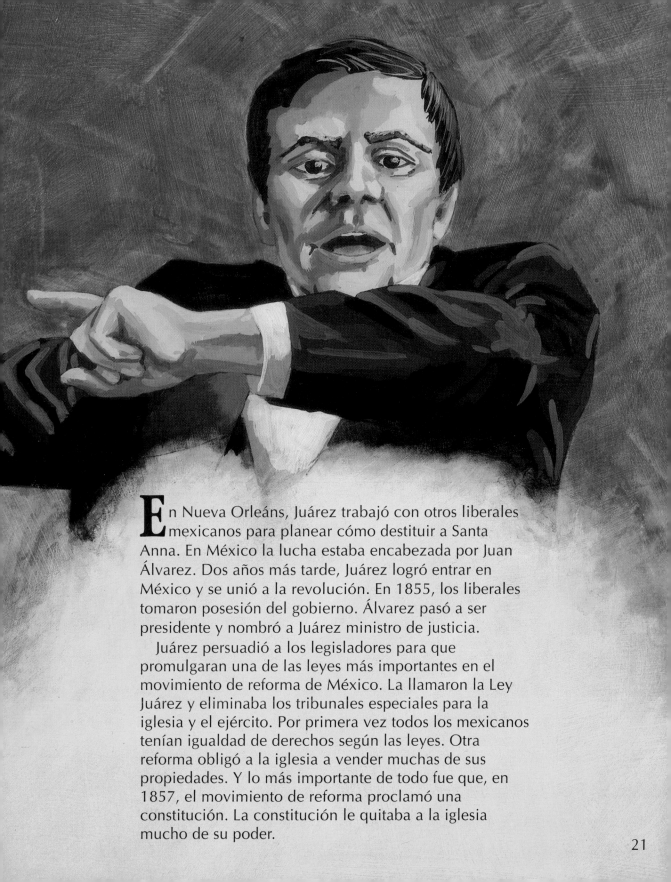

En Nueva Orleáns, Juárez trabajó con otros liberales mexicanos para planear cómo destituir a Santa Anna. En México la lucha estaba encabezada por Juan Álvarez. Dos años más tarde, Juárez logró entrar en México y se unió a la revolución. En 1855, los liberales tomaron posesión del gobierno. Álvarez pasó a ser presidente y nombró a Juárez ministro de justicia.

Juárez persuadió a los legisladores para que promulgaran una de las leyes más importantes en el movimiento de reforma de México. La llamaron la Ley Juárez y eliminaba los tribunales especiales para la iglesia y el ejército. Por primera vez todos los mexicanos tenían igualdad de derechos según las leyes. Otra reforma obligó a la iglesia a vender muchas de sus propiedades. Y lo más importante de todo fue que, en 1857, el movimiento de reforma proclamó una constitución. La constitución le quitaba a la iglesia mucho de su poder.

In 1857, a new president was elected. Juárez was chosen to head the supreme court, which also made him the vice-president. In 1858, the church and the army started a revolution. The president fled to the United States, and Juárez went to Guanajuato. According to the constitution, he was now the president of Mexico, so he claimed that the legal government was in Guanajuato. This was the beginning of a civil war that lasted three years.

Some of the leaders of Juárez's army quit, and others went over to the enemy's side. However, Benito Juárez was an energetic and stubborn man. He just did not give up, and the people's support for him grew day by day. Juárez's army slowly gained strength and won the war. Juárez returned to Mexico City as the legal president on January 11, 1861, but this was not the end of Mexico's problems.

En 1857 un nuevo presidente fue elegido. A Juárez lo escogieron para dirigir la corte suprema, lo cual significaba que era también vice presidente. En 1858, la iglesia y el ejército iniciaron una revolución. El presidente huyó a los Estados Unidos y Juárez fue a Guanajuato. De acuerdo con la constitución, él era ahora el presidente de México. Por esta razón declaró que el gobierno estaba en Guanajuato. Así comenzó una guerra civil que duró tres años.

Algunos de los oficiales del ejército de Juárez renunciaron y otros se pasaron al enemigo. Sin embargo, Benito Juárez era un hombre enérgico y tenaz. No se dio por vencido, y cada día aumentaba el apoyo que recibía del pueblo. El ejército de Juárez cobró fuerza poco a poco y ganó la guerra. Juárez regresó a la ciudad de México como presidente legal, el 11 de enero de 1861, pero los problemas de México no habían terminado.

The Mexican government had almost no money, and it owed a large amount to other countries. England, France, and Spain decided to send armies to collect the debt. They invited the United States to join them, but President Abraham Lincoln angrily refused. Soon after landing in Mexico, the British and Spanish soldiers went home, but the French stayed. The leader of France, Emperor Napoleon III, wanted to take over Mexico. When the French army reached Mexico City, Juárez had to flee. The French set up a government with the Mexican Conservatives and brought in Maximilian of Austria to be the emperor. Mexico was now a monarchy.

El gobierno mexicano no tenía casi nada de dinero y les debía mucho dinero a otras naciones. Inglaterra, Francia y España decidieron enviar ejércitos para cobrar la deuda. Le pidieron a los Estados Unidos que se uniera a ellos, pero el presidente Abraham Lincoln se negó rotundamente. Poco después de desembarcar en México, los soldados ingleses y españoles regresaron a sus países, pero los franceses se quedaron. El emperador Napoleón III quería apoderarse de México. Cuando el ejército francés llegó a la ciudad de México, Juárez tuvo que huir. Los franceses establecieron un gobierno con los conservadores mexicanos y nombraron a Maximiliano de Austria para que fuera emperador. México pasó a ser una monarquía.

Maximilian's army was fighting the small Mexican army led by Porfirio Díaz. Juárez had moved north and was also fighting Maximilian. The emperor had other troubles. For one thing, his government was running out of money. Also, Napoleon III was worried that the United States would get involved in the fighting.

In 1867, Napoleon decided to take the French soldiers out of Mexico. The Mexican Conservatives fought on, but they were defeated. Maximilian and the two top Conservative generals were captured and killed.

El ejército de Maximiliano luchaba contra el pequeño ejército mexicano al mando de Porfirio Díaz. Juárez se había ido al norte y también luchaba contra Maximiliano. El emperador tenía otros problemas. De una parte, su gobierno se estaba quedando sin dinero. Por otra parte, Napoleón III temía que los Estados Unidos interviniera en la contienda.

En 1867, Napoleón decidió sacar de México a los soldados franceses. Los conservadores mexicanos pelearon, pero fueron derrotados. Maximiliano y los dos generales conservadores de mayor poder fueron capturados y ejecutados.

Benito Juárez returned to Mexico City. He had gained his country's respect and admiration for his activities. In that same year, 1867, Juárez was re-elected president. The wars were over, but Mexico's problems were still enormous. The country and most of its people were very poor. There was little industry and almost no trade with other countries. Few of the people were educated. Many men, who had spent their entire lives as soldiers and now had nothing to do, became bandits and roamed the countryside.

Benito Juárez regresó a la ciudad de México. Se había ganado el respeto y la admiración de su país por sus acciones. En ese mismo año, 1867, Juárez fue reelegido presidente. Las guerras habían terminado, pero los problemas de México eran todavía enormes. El país y la mayoría de su gente eran muy pobres. Había muy poca industria y muy poco comercio con otros países. Muy pocas de las personas tenían educación. Muchos hombres, que se habían pasado la vida de soldados y ahora no tenían nada que hacer, se volvieron bandidos y asaltantes en los campos.

In the four years of Juárez's term of office, he went a long way toward making the government strong. Some people thought he made the government too strong and that he was becoming a dictator. When he was re-elected in 1871, the results were so close that congress had to decide who won. Then, Porfirio Díaz led a revolt against his old friend. The revolt was put down, but it was a bad way for Juárez to start a new term as president.

On July 18, 1872, Benito Juárez had a heart attack. His doctor ordered him to bed, but Juárez worked quietly until he died, just before midnight.

Benito Juárez was a brilliant, stubborn, honest, and simple man who wanted one thing. He wanted to improve the lives of the people of Mexico. More than any person before or since, he accomplished that goal.

Durante sus cuatro años de gobierno, Juárez se esforzó por fortalecer el gobierno. Algunas personas pensaban que le daba demasiados poderes al gobierno y que se estaba convirtiendo en un dictador. Cuando fue reelegido en 1871 los resultados de la votación fueron tan semejantes para los dos candidatos, que el congreso tuvo que decidir quién había ganado. Entonces Porfirio Díaz encabezó una revuelta en contra de su viejo amigo. La revuelta fue controlada, pero era un mal comienzo para el nuevo período de Juárez como presidente.

El 18 de julio de 1872, Benito Juárez sufrió un ataque al corazón. El médico lo mandó a la cama, pero él se quedó trabajando tranquilamente hasta que murió, cerca de la medianoche.

Benito Juárez fue un hombre brillante, tenaz, honesto y sencillo que quería una cosa. Quería mejorar la vida de los mexicanos. Y nadie jamás, antes o después, ha cumplido esa meta mejor que él.

GLOSSARY

civil war A clash between opposing groups of citizens in the same country.

constitution The basic laws of a nation.

dictator An individual who holds complete power over a country.

legislature The lawmaking body of a government.

monarchy The rule of a country by a king, emperor, or other royal leader.

reform The removal or correction of an abuse or a wrong.

revolt The attempted overthrow of a government.

GLOSARIO

constitución Las leyes básicas de una nación.

dictador Individuo que tiene completo poder sobre un país.

guerra civil Lucha entre dos grupos opuestos de los ciudadanos de un mismo país.

legislatura Cuerpo de legisladores, que dictan las leyes de un país.

monarquía Gobierno de un país por un rey, emperador u otra figura real.

reforma Eliminación o corrección de un abuso o falta.

revuelta Intento de deponer a un gobierno.

TOTALLY AWESOME PUZZLES

First published 2016 by Parragon Books, Ltd.

Copyright © 2018 Cottage Door Press, LLC
5005 Newport Drive
Rolling Meadows, Illinois 60008

ISBN: 978-1-68052-414-7

Parragon Books is an imprint of Cottage Door Press, LLC.
Parragon Books® and the Parragon® logo are
registered trademarks of Cottage Door Press, LLC.

Written by Claire Sipi and Susan Fairbrother
Illustrated by Emily Golden, Beatrice Costamagna, Dean Gray, and Matthew Scott

TOTALLY AWESOME PUZZLES

PaRragon.

Follow these directions to find the treasure!

START

5

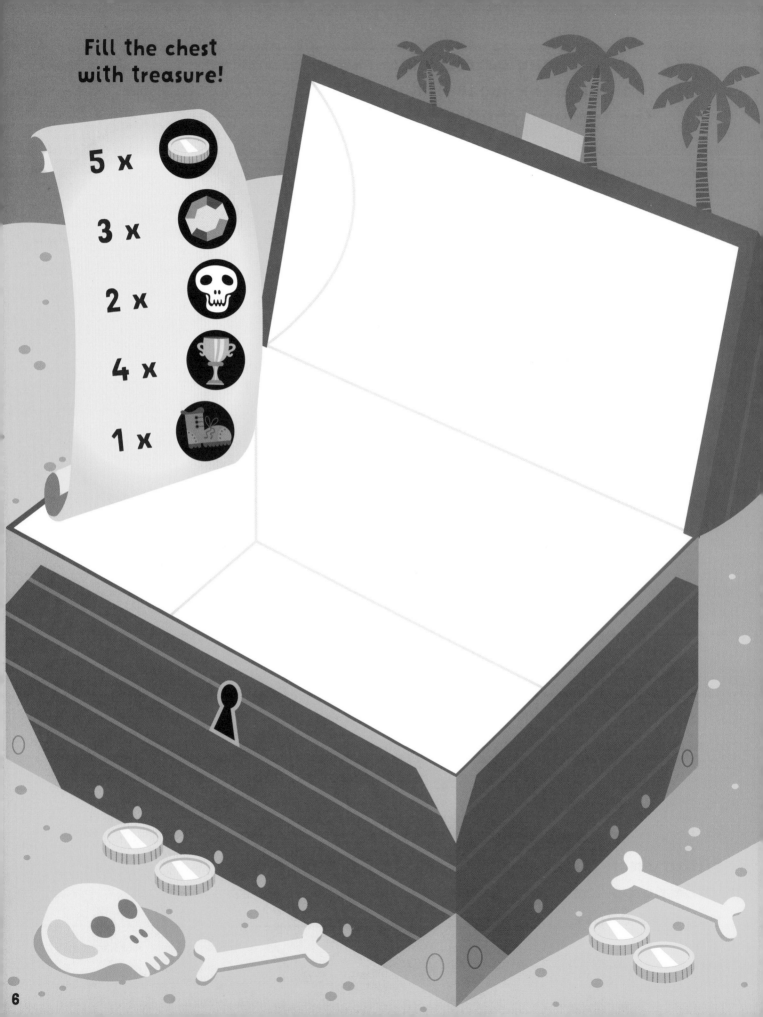

Fill the chest with treasure!

5 x
3 x
2 x
4 x
1 x

6

Arrr, we missed! Where do our next **4** tries land?

Use these coordinates to find out!

~~B2~~ C5 A4 D1 E2

Fill in each blank club by adding up the numbers in the balls on either side.

11

Time to spread some joy!
Now ... who do I need to find?

2 grumpy gnomes ☐

3 frustrated fairies ☐

4 unhappy elves ☐

14

15

FINISH

Pitch these tents in the right order by adding the missing numbers!

2   6   8

10   15   25

1   4   5

Can you help us finish serving the food?

Each plate should add up to **8**.

Draw the missing food items on the plates.

19

Fill in each blank by adding up
the two numbers above it—then run!

Draw lines to match each dino with its nest.

Hmm ... which nest is mine? I laid **10** eggs.

I laid **2** eggs fewer than Green Grace.

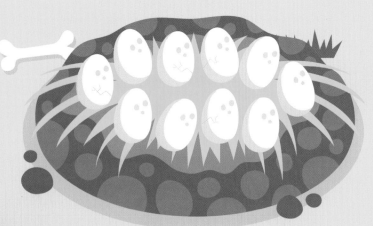

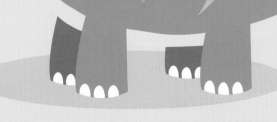

22

23

Help us build the pyramids by filling in the missing numbers.

Fill in each blank by adding up the numbers in the triangles on either side.

Thieves have taken **10** items from the pharaoh's tomb!

26

What's missing?

Follow these directions to rescue the Duke!

FINISH

START

Caw! Use the color key to finish the dragon.

29

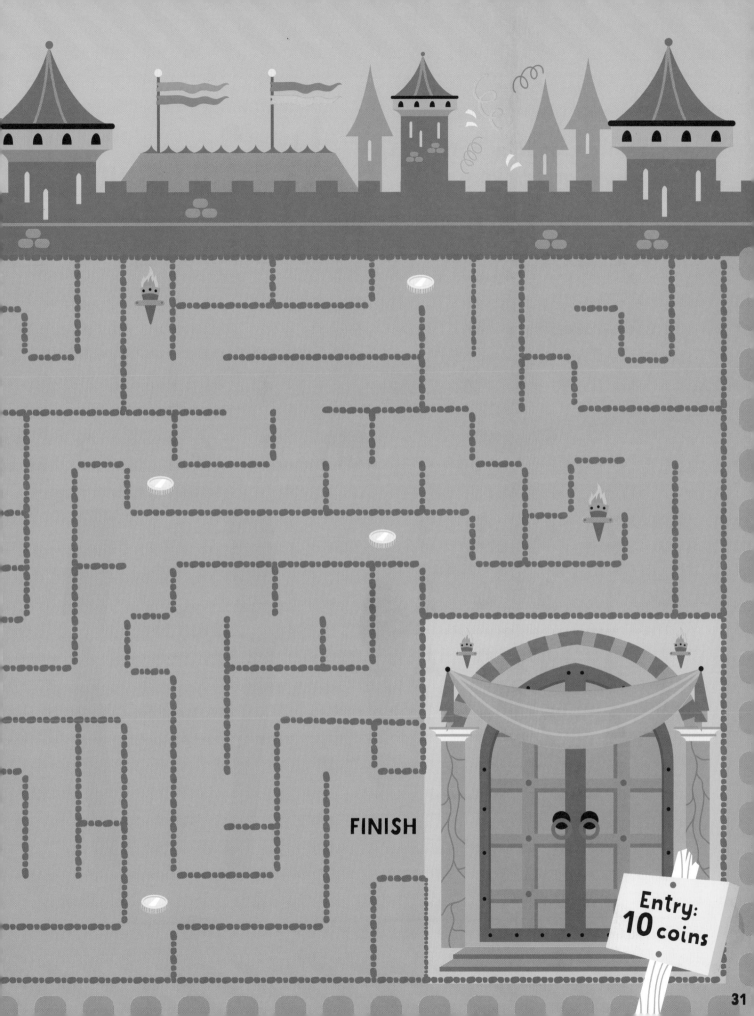

FINISH

Entry:
10 coins

31

5	8	7	3	4	6
2	1	9	7	5	2
4	6	8	3	9	3
5	6	4	2	1	3
3	9	8	6	5	6
7	1	2	3	4	9

Find these numbers:
123, 975, 246, 369.
Search up, down, forward, and backward!

START

FINISH

Hmm ... Which is the correct answer to finish my machine?

Add up the numbers in the machine to figure out which answer should plug in! Circle the correct answer.

11   12   13

35

How many fans does each monster have?

My fans have brought banners! I've got

_____ fans.

My fans are wearing hats! I've got

_____ fans.

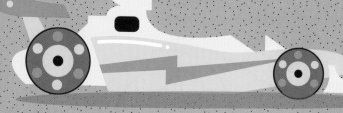

My fans are waving flags! I've got

_____ fans.

Car color	Lap time (seconds)			
	1	+ 2	+ 3	= Total
Yellow	5	+ 10	+ 10	=
Orange	10	+ 5	+ 5	=
Green	10	+ 10	+ 10	=

... And they've done it! Add up the lap times to find the fastest and slowest times, then color the cars in the right colors.

I was the slowest ... but I had fun!

38

START

FINISH

Do you think Goat
will go through
the check points in
the right order?

Ride these cable cars
in the right order by adding
the missing numbers!

43

Look at what I've built!

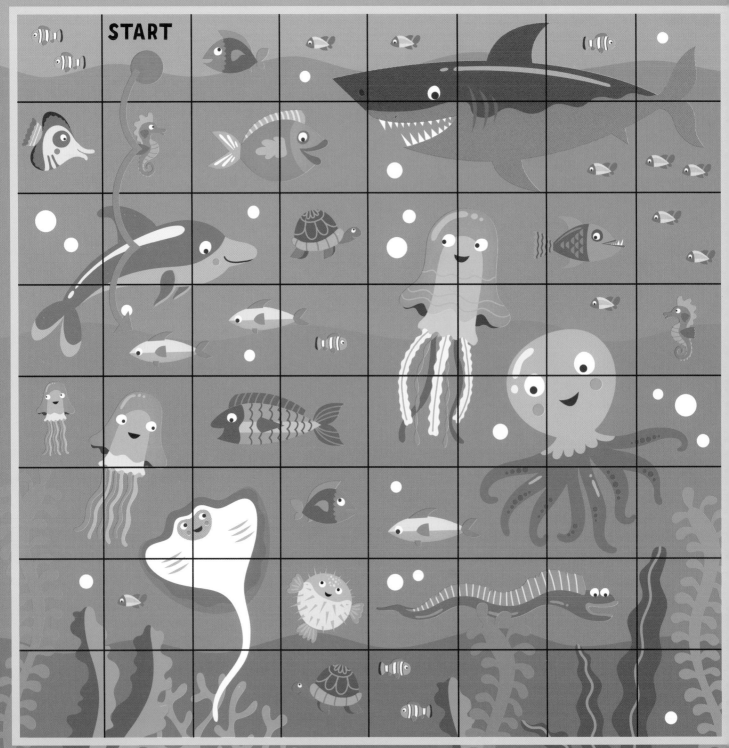

Follow these directions to find the rare puffer fish!

START

Use the color key to finish the picture.

1 2 3 4 5

49

10 sea creatures have left the reef for warmer waters!

Who's missing?

53

START

Go up, down, left, or right at the odd-numbered houses to get the delivery driver to the right house.

54

 1
 5
 7
 3
 8

 3
 4
 6
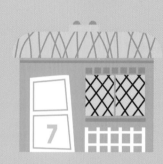 7
 2

 9
 6
 5
 3
 2

 5
 2
 5

I'm getting really hungry!

FINISH

 8
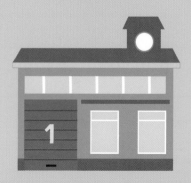 1
 7
 9

55

56

Caw! Fill in each blank by adding up the two numbers below it.

59

Bug spotter's guide:

2 black spiders ☐

1 red butterfly ☐

5 yellow dragonflies ☐

3 blue bugs ☐

8 green grasshoppers ☐

62

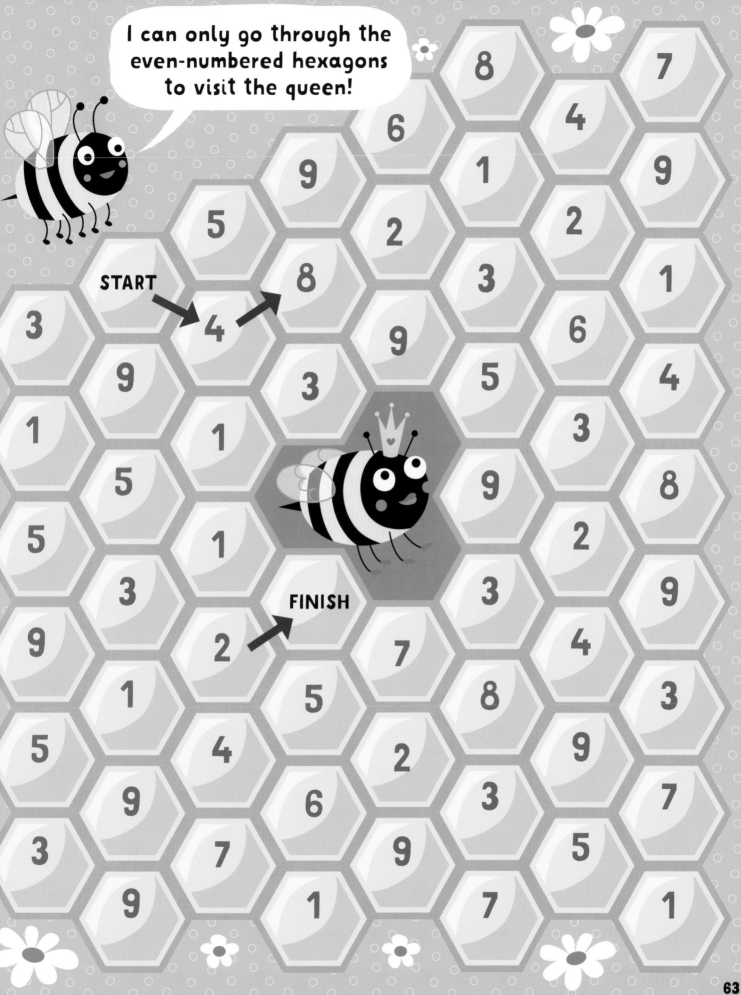

WINTER

Brrr! Which birds have flown away?

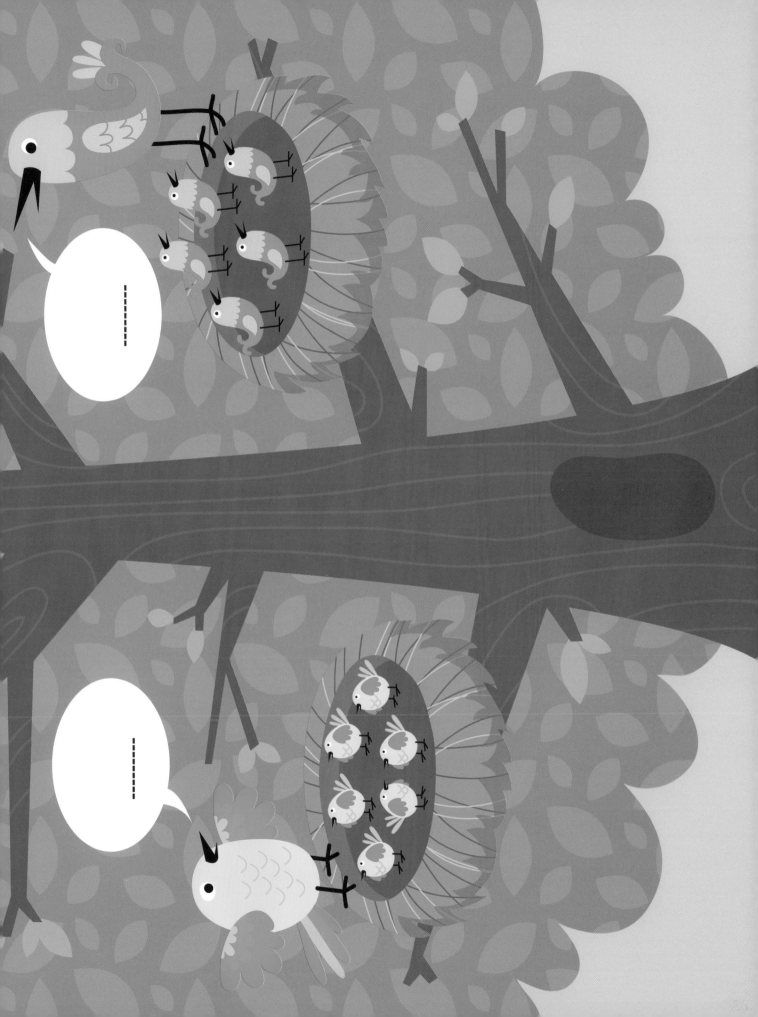

4

The monkeys took my glasses, too! What's peeping out of the leaves?

Use the color key to finish the picture.

1 2 3 4 5

71

It's nice to meet you! What are your names?

You can guess! We'll each give a clue to someone else's name.

Coral is holding **1** pink comb and has **2** orange starfish in her hair.

My name is

Star has **3** stars on his top and **6** red scales on his tail.

My name is

Pebble has **7** spots on his top and **1** strand of seaweed in his hair.

Madison has **2** shells in her hair.

My name is

My name is

Shelley has **4** green shells in her hair and a necklace with **5** purple jewels.

My name is

Use the color key to finish the picture.

75

14-5-24-20   20-1-18-7-5-20

N
------------------- -------------------

9-19   20-8-5   2-1-14-11
------------------- ------------------- -------------------

Quick! We need to decode this secret message to find the robber's next target!

I have the code breaker here!

A = 1	B = 2	C = 3	D = 4
E = 5	F = 6	G = 7	H = 8
I = 9	J = 10	K = 11	L = 12
M = 13	N = 14	O = 15	P = 16
Q = 17	R = 18	S = 19	T = 20
U = 21	V = 22	X = 24	
Y = 25	Z = 26	W = 23	

Add up the minutes it takes to drive down each road to find the quickest route to the bank!

Red route: _____ Blue route: _____

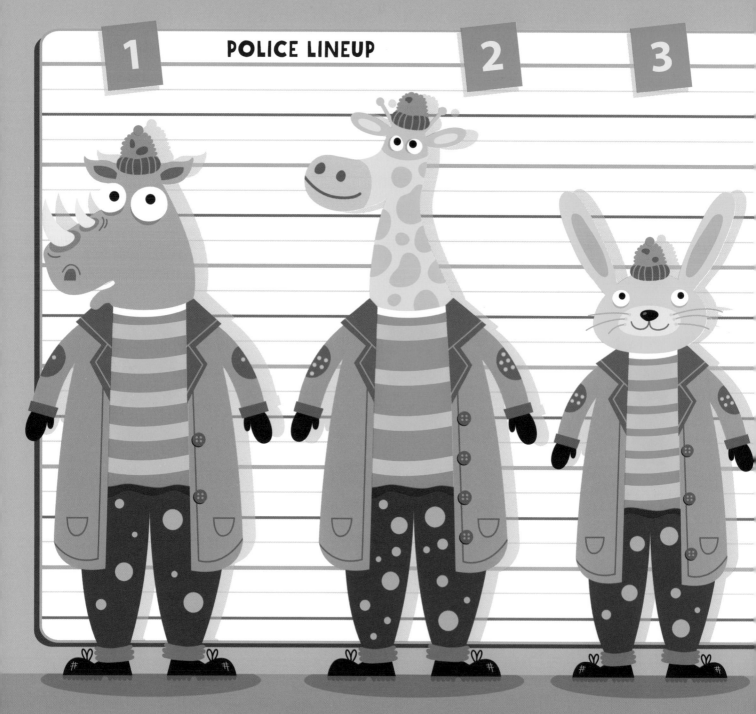

Read the witness accounts to find the robber.

The robber had **1** pom-pom on his hat!

There were **7** spots on his pants!

The robber had **3** buttons on his coat!

| 4 | 5 | 6 |

There were **4** spots on each elbow pad.

He had **5** orange stripes on his t-shirt!

It was number

_____ !

Draw lines to join up the coordinates to reveal the sacred temple!

B4 → D4 → D3 → G6 → D9 → D8 → B8 → B4

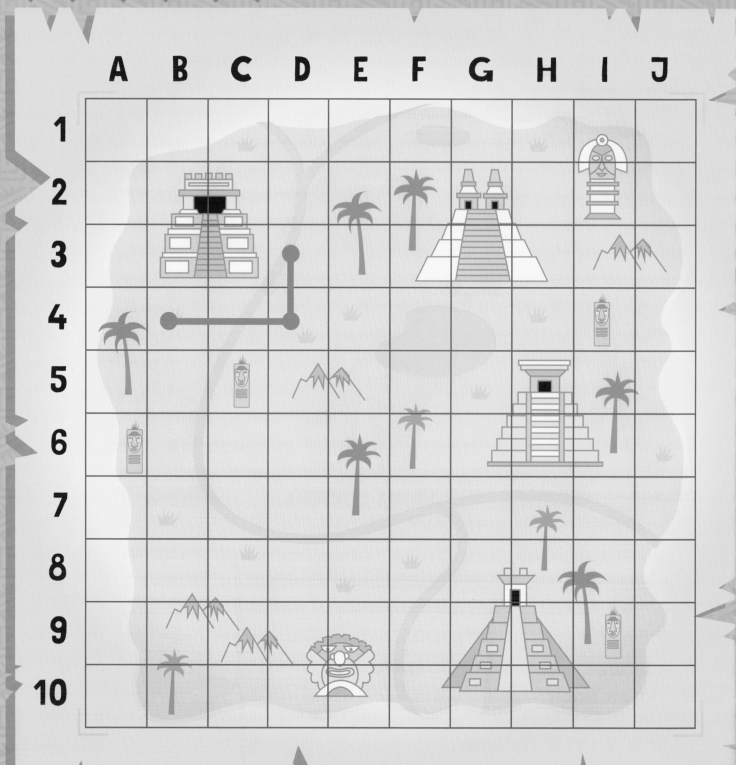

Use the code below to
find the answers and
unlock the temple door!

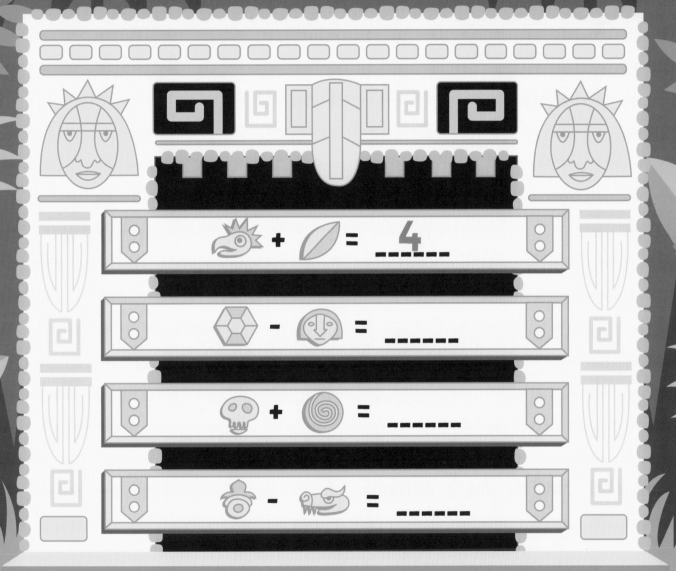

8 + 7 - 6 =

8   9

FINISH

**Phew! The house is almost finished.
It should look exactly like these plans.**

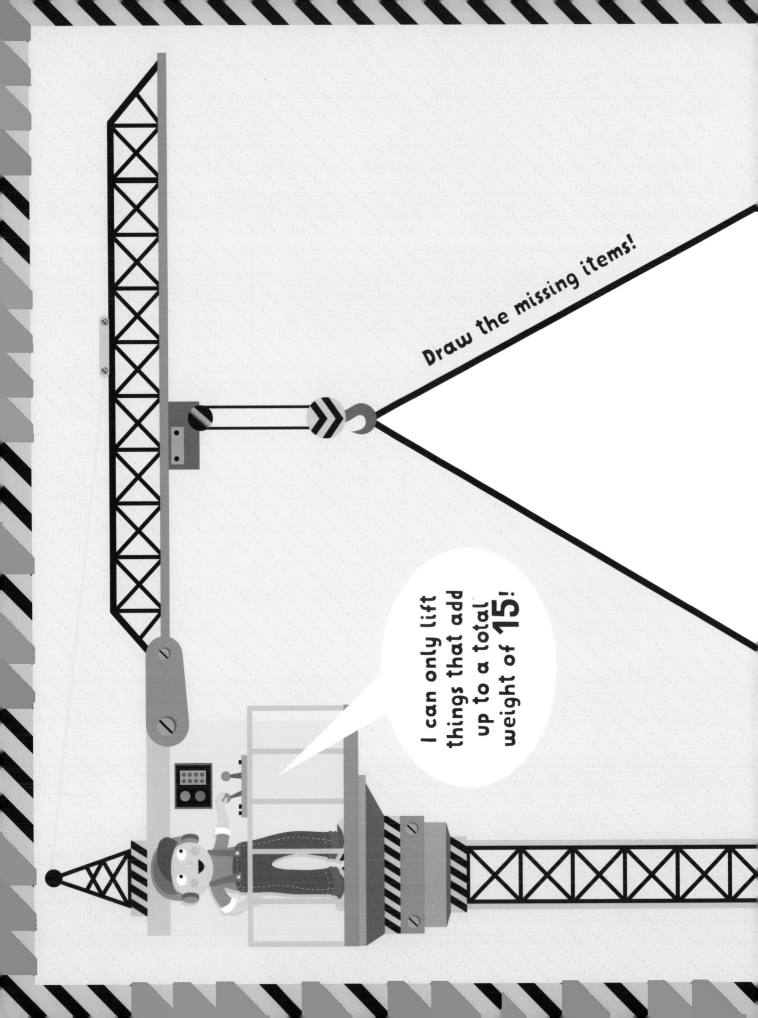

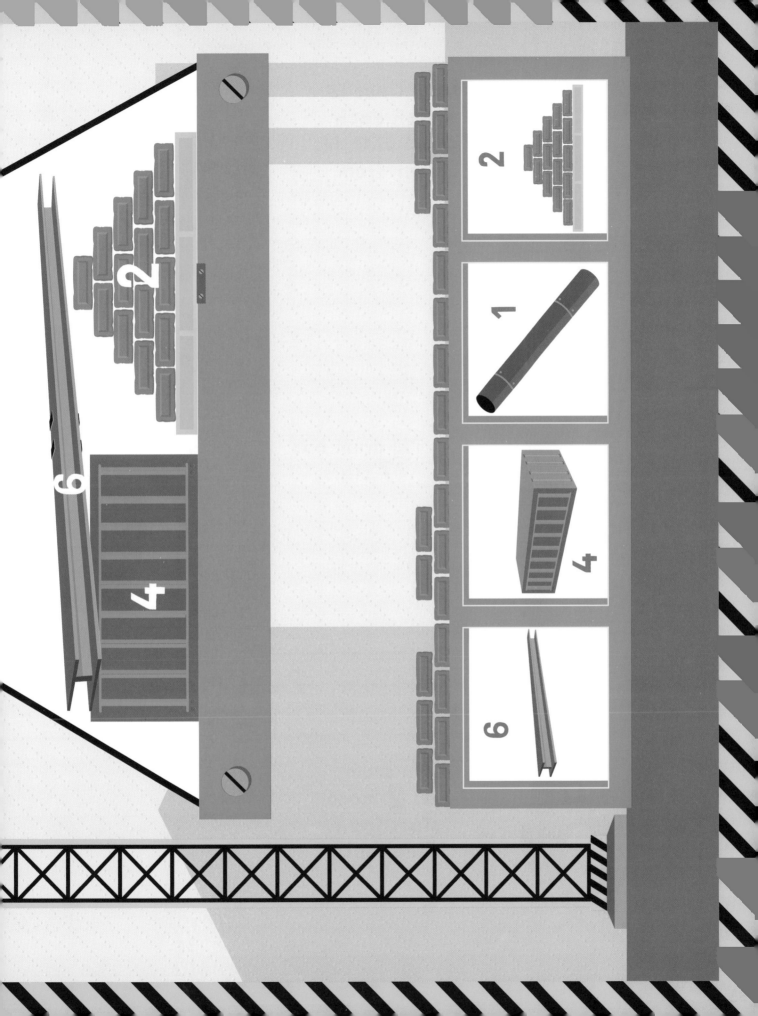

START

PARADE ROUTE:

Pass **4** houses,
each with **2** windows.

Pass **2** shops selling vegetables.

Pass the fire station.

Pass **2** parked blue cars.

Pass **3** restaurants.

Pass **5** parked red cars.

Pass the café.

Where does the parade end?

_____

VEGETABLES

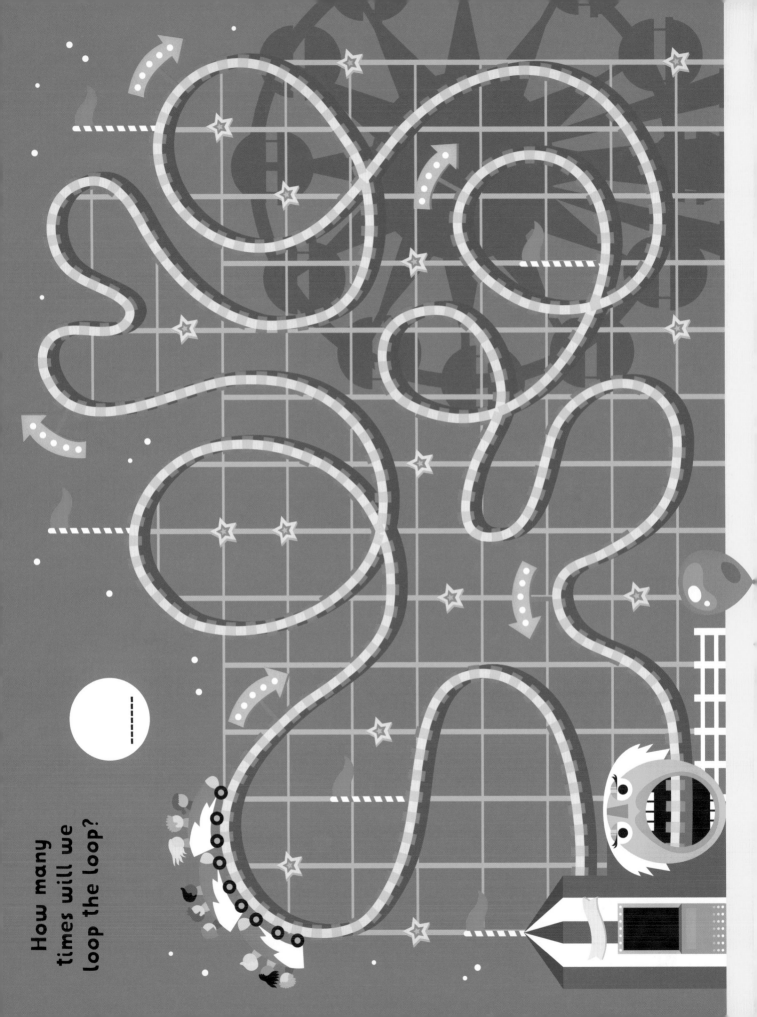

How many times will we loop the loop?

Who will win the trophy?

I won all the even-numbered prizes! How many did I get?

---------- even prizes

95

FINISH

100

Fit the numbers below into the grid to help me find the new computer code (the numbers in the red squares).

38762
17395
52729
65284
3413526
2954984

Follow these coordinates to land the spacecraft.

C2 - B2 - B5 - D5 - D6 - E6 - E8

FINISH

104

Add up the score cards to find the highest and lowest scores, then write in the names of each pair.

Alex and Ava 
8 7 7 9
TOTAL:
....

Gavin and Grace 
9 8 8 8
TOTAL:
....

Liam and Lily 
7 8 8 9
TOTAL:
....

108

FINISH

FINISH

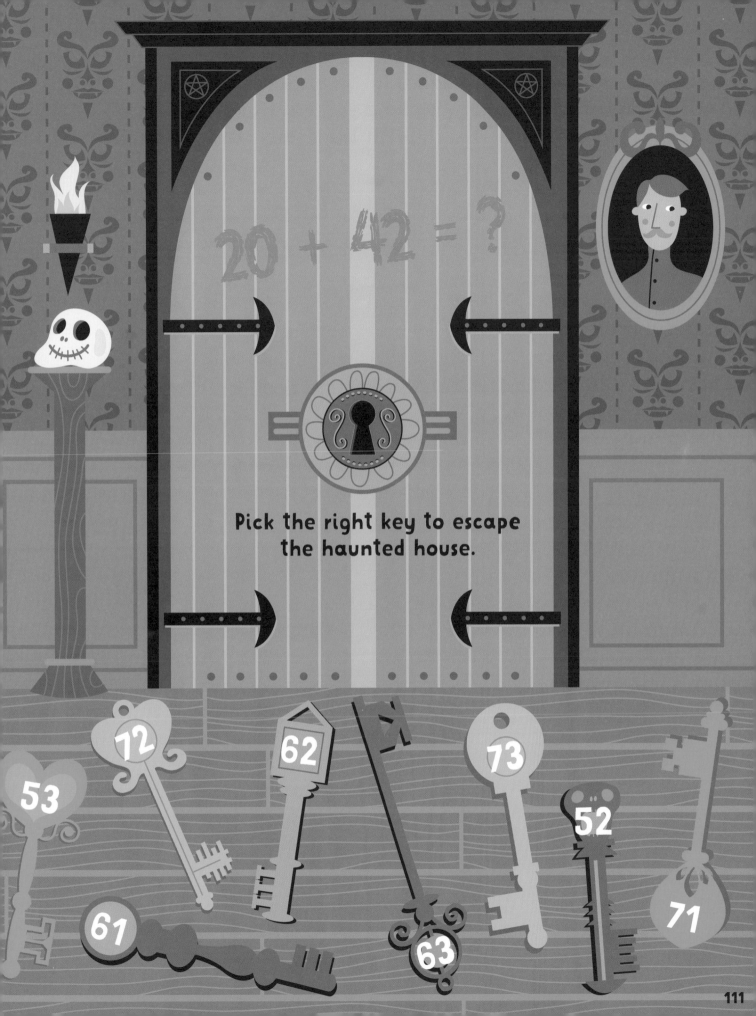

20 + 42 = ?

Pick the right key to escape the haunted house.

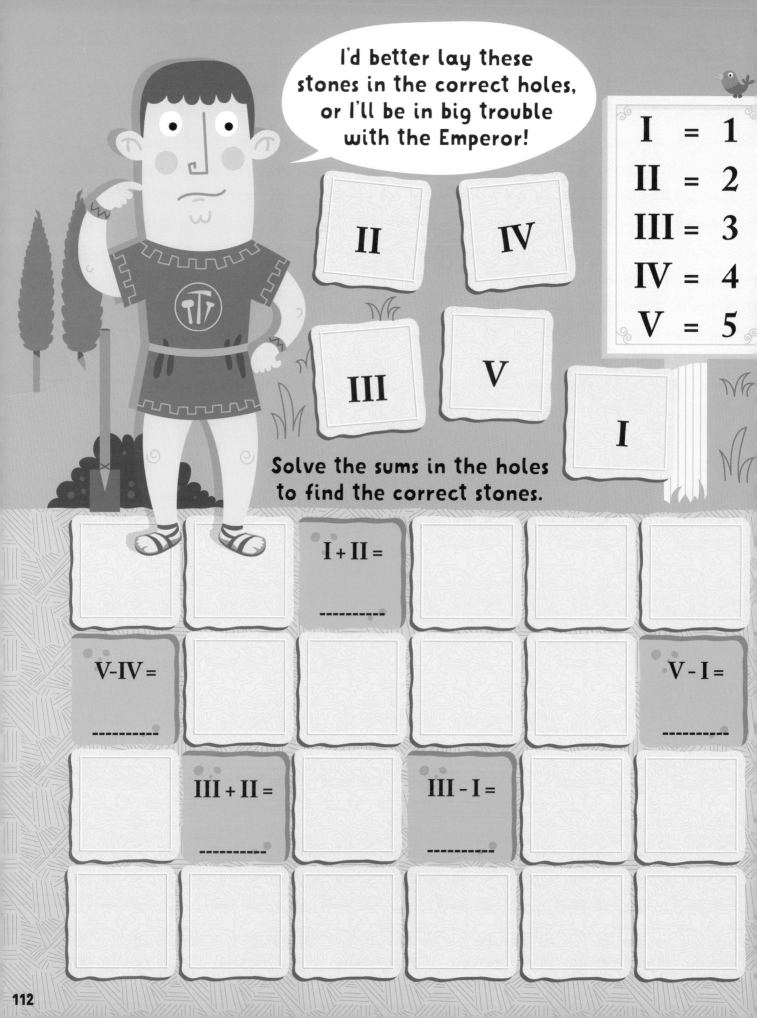

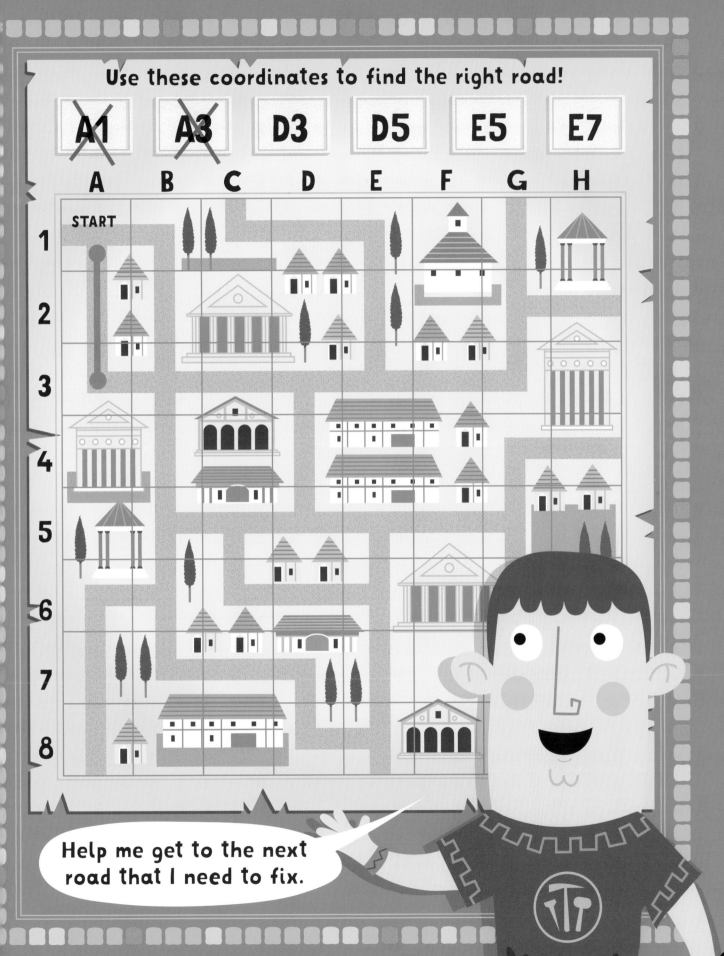

113

114

Help each passenger find his or her platform!

DEPARTURES		PLATFORM
10:45	Greenville	4
10:50	Springfield	5
10:55	Madison	7
11:00	Franklin	2
11:10	Washington	1
11:15	Salem	8
CURRENT TIME:		10:40

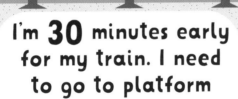

10:40

My train leaves in **5** minutes! I need to go to platform

....

I'm **30** minutes early for my train. I need to go to platform

....

My train leaves in **15** minutes. I need to go to platform

....

I'm **20** minutes early for my train. I need to go to platform

....

Play this game with a friend!

You will need:
2 counters + 1 die

How to play:

1. Each player puts their counter on the START square.

2. Take turns rolling the die. Move your counter forward the number of spaces shown on the die.

3. If your counter lands at the bottom of a hurdle, you can move up to the top of the hurdle.

4. The first player to get to the FINISH square is the winner.

FINISH 48	47	46
33	34	35
32	31	30
17	18	19
16	15	14
START 1	2	3

45	44	43	42	41
36	37	38	39	40
29	28	27	26	25
20	21	22	23	24
13	12	11	10	9
4	5	6	7	8

ANSWERS

Pages 4-5

Pages 6-7

Pages 8-9
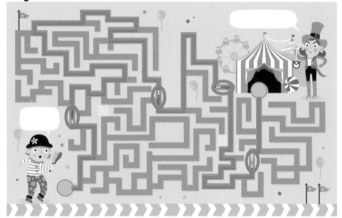

Pages 10-11

Pages 12-13

Pages 14-15

Pages 16-17

Pages 18-19

Pages 20-21

Pages 22-23

Pages 24-25

Pages 26-27

Pages 28-29

Pages 30-31

Pages 32-33

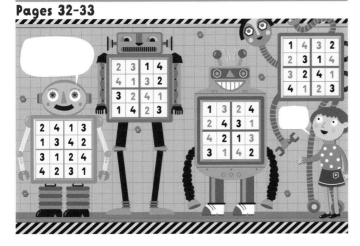

Pages 34-35

123

Pages 36-37

Pages 38-39

Pages 40-41

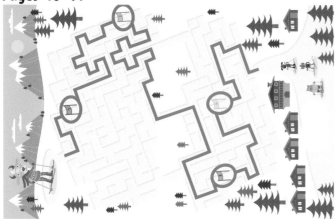

Pages 42-43

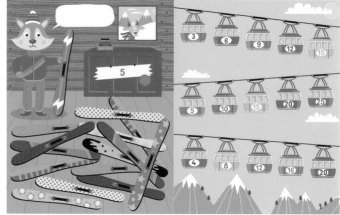

Pages 44-45

Pages 46-47

Pages 48-49

Pages 50-51

Pages 52-53

Pages 54-55

Pages 56-57

Pages 58-59

Pages 60-61

Pages 62-63

Pages 64-65

Pages 66-67

Pages 68-69

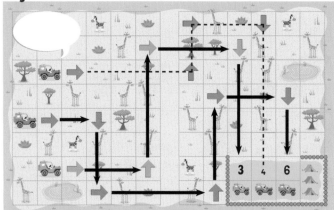

Pages 70-71

Pages 72-73

Pages 74-75

Pages 76-77

Pages 78-79

Pages 80-81

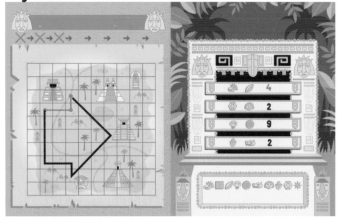

Pages 82-83

Pages 84-85

Pages 86-87

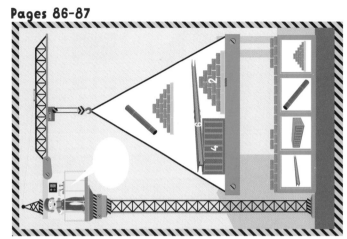

Pages 88-89

Pages 90-91

Pages 92-93

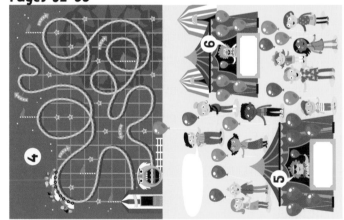

Pages 94-95

Pages 96-97

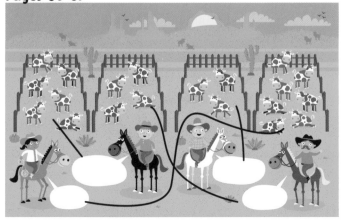

Pages 98-99

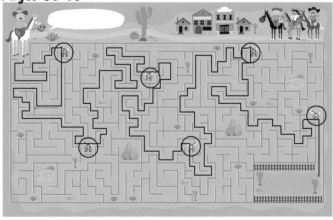

127

Pages 100-101

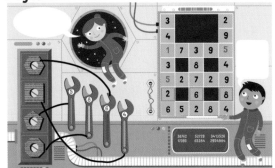

Pages 102-103

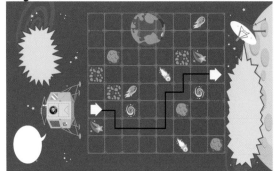

Pages 104-105

Pages 106-107

Pages 108-109

Pages 110-111

Pages 112-113

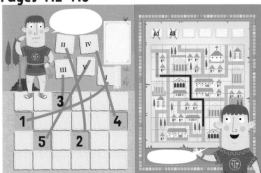

Pages 114-115

Pages 116-117

Pages 118-119

LOTS AND LOTS OF DOT-TO-DOTS

What's going on
at the farm?

Arrr! Treasure ahoy!

134

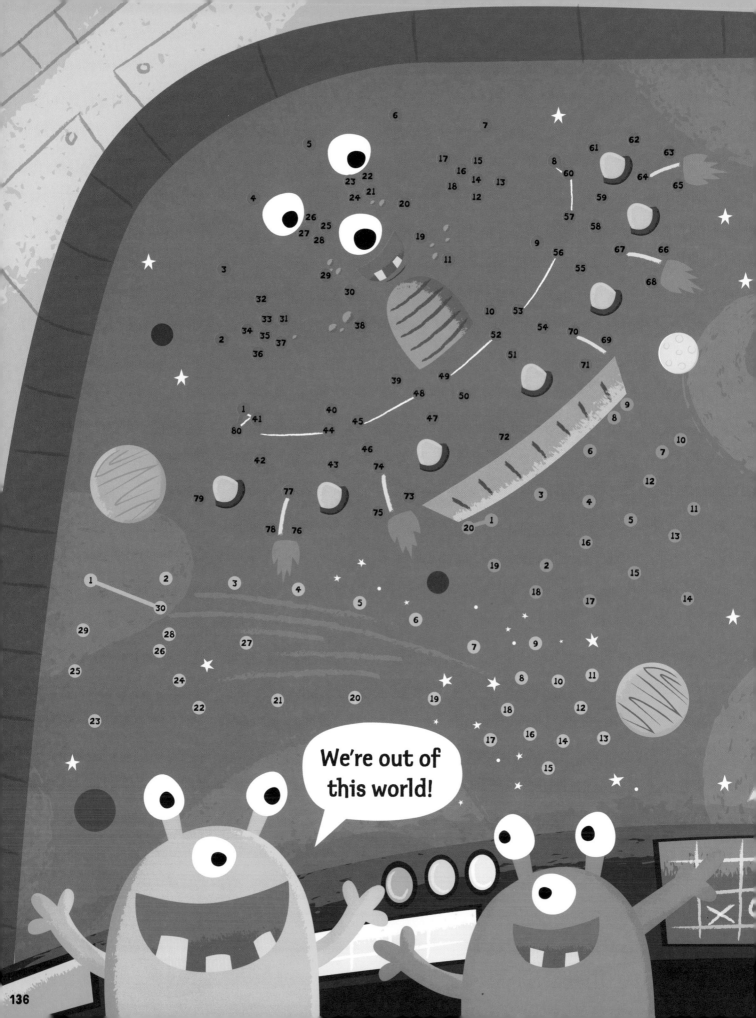

Make a wish ...

138

Crack!

Crack!

Crack!

140

Crack!

Hello, world!

141

The garden's full of
creepy-crawlies.

144

What can you see beside the sea?

145

That's not Grandma ...

147

Everybody freeze!

151

Practice makes perfect.

152

154

Spot the dot-to-dot odd one out.

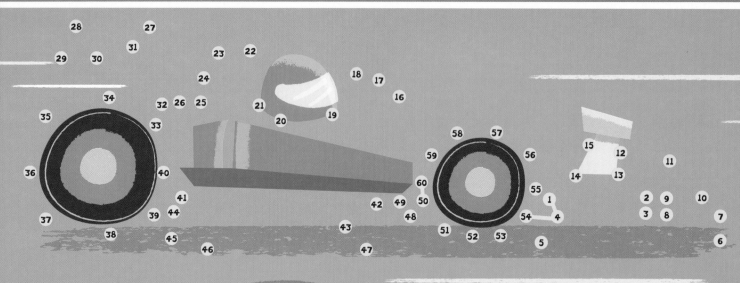

Take a trip under the ocean.

Let's get busy building.

164

They're friendly!

It's the great Stupendo!
He can read minds …

Boing!
Boing!

173

Everyone's on the move.

Once upon a time, in a tumbledown castle, there lived ...

Roar!

Let's finish the other half.

Hissss!

There's plenty to share!

186

Look at all the animals!

188

There's fairy dust everywhere.

Zooooom!

What a mess!

I think they've made friends.

196

198

I don't know what you are ...

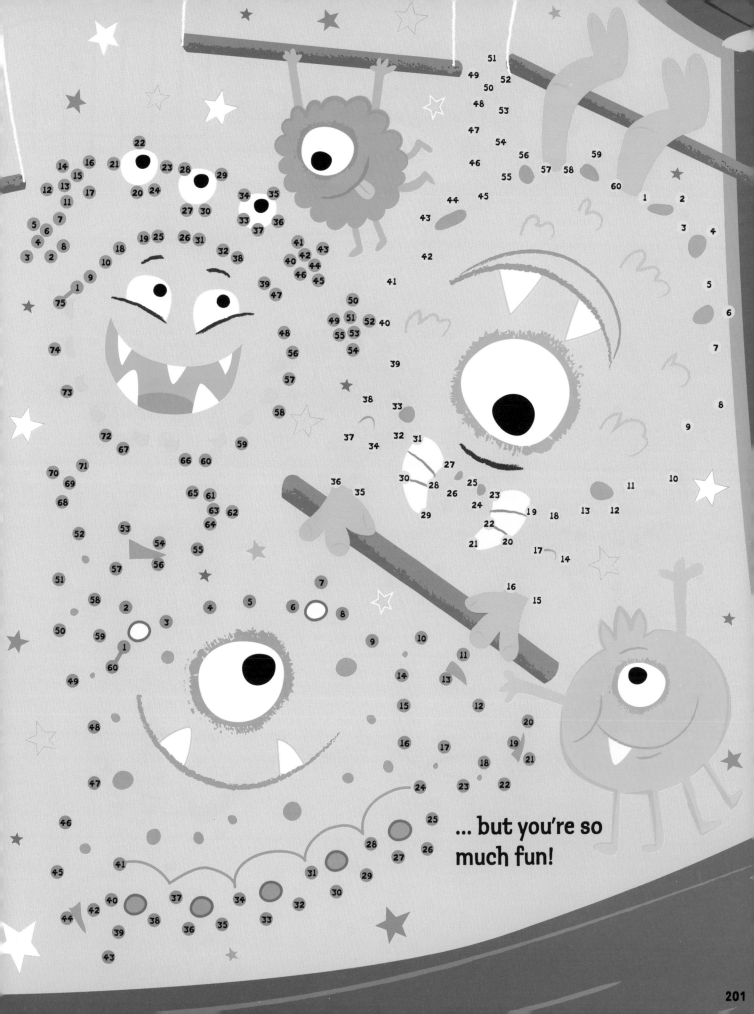

... but you're so much fun!

201

Every Viking needs a helmet.

205

Whee!

206

Who do you think lives here?

208

Eek!

Make my garden grow.

212

213

Take a twirl.

214

216

Where are we?

217

We love playing in the snow!

218

Snip Snip

A new hairdo for you?

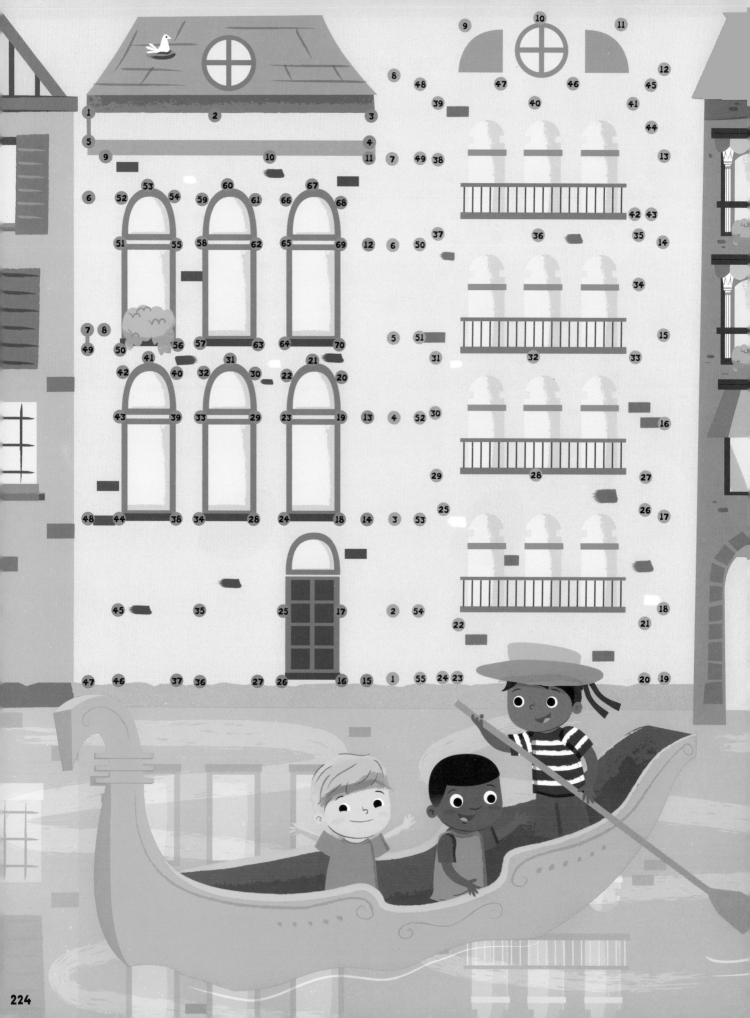

There's lots to
see on this tour.

Mirror, mirror, on the wall ...

... who's the fairest of them all?

Watch your step!

228

229

Spot which dot-to-dot animals are lost.

Boo!

234

235

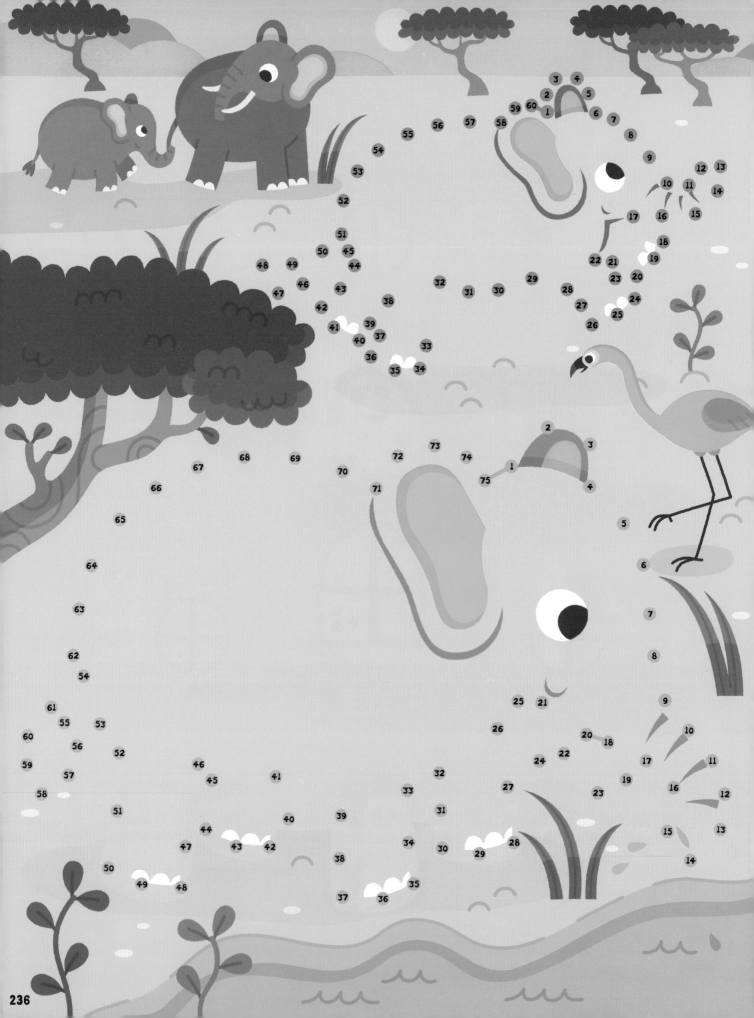

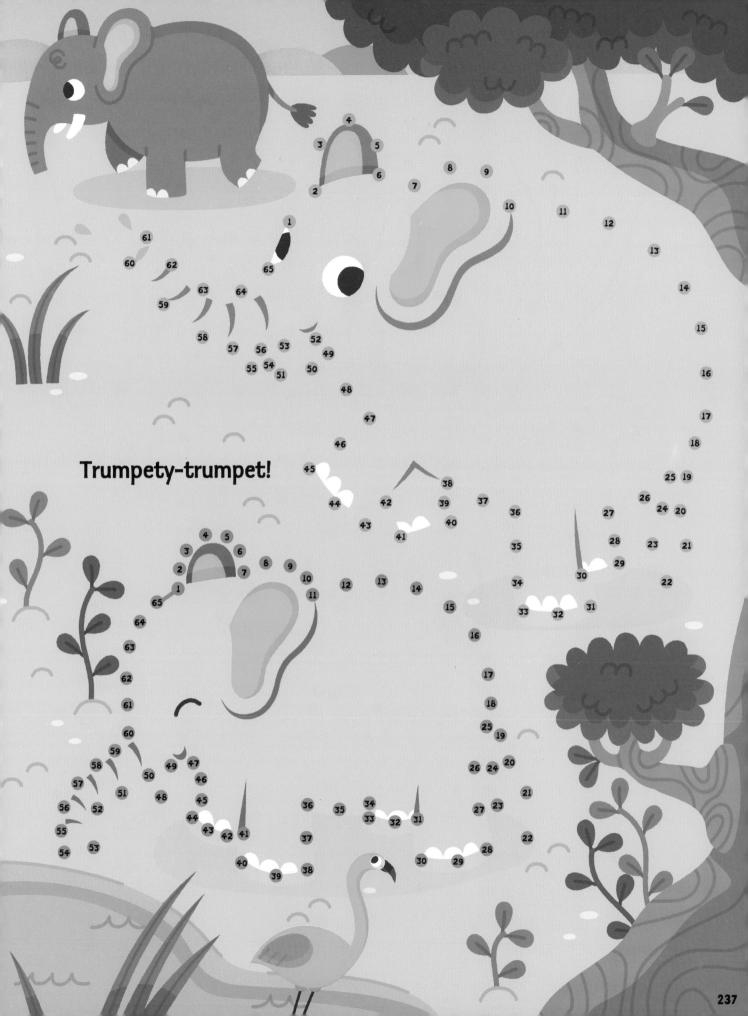

Trumpety-trumpet!

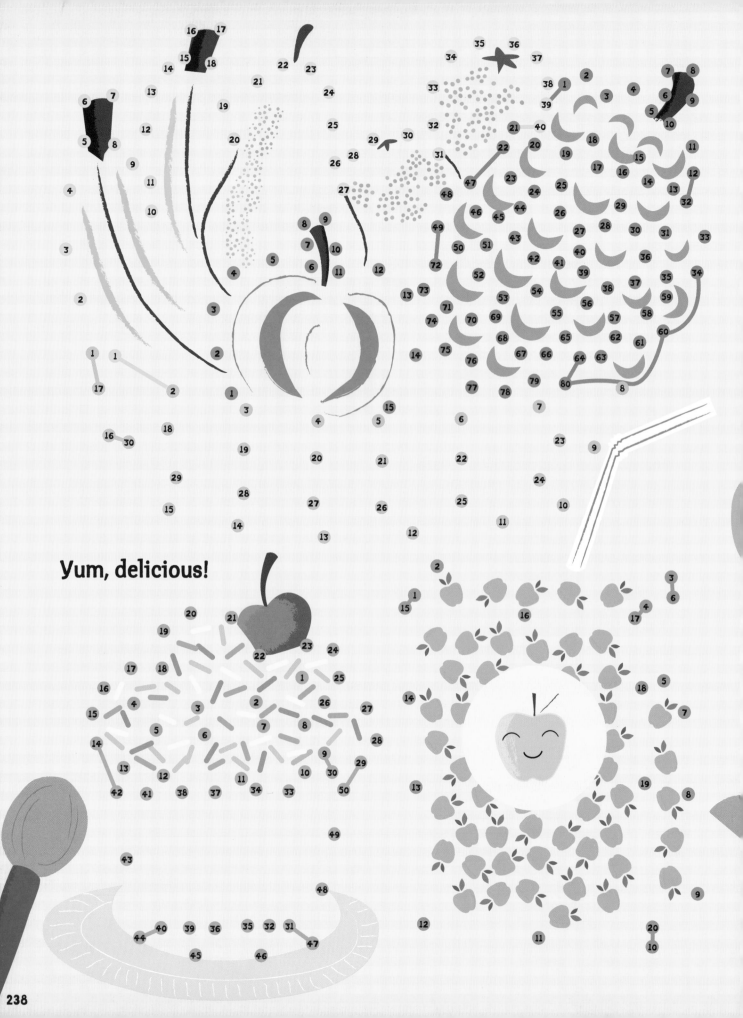

Yum, delicious!

Welcome to the big city.

Be a fashion designer! Dot-to-dot some super-stylish outfits.

This is awesome!

Join the dots ... if you're feeling brave!

Flap

Flap

Flap

Solutions

Pages 132-133

Pages 134-135

Pages 136-137

Pages 138-139

Pages 140-141

Pages 142-143

Pages 144-145

Pages 146-147

Pages 148-149

Pages 150-151

Pages 152-153

Pages 154-155

Pages 156-157

Pages 158-159

Pages 160-161

Pages 162-163

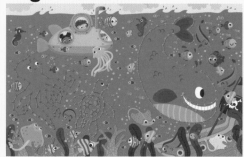

Pages 164-165

Pages 166-167

Pages 168-169

Pages 170-171

Pages 172-173

Pages 174-175

Pages 176-177

Pages 178-179

Pages 180-181

Pages 182-183

Pages 184-185

Pages 186-187

Pages 188-189

Pages 190-191

Pages 192-193

Pages 194-195

Pages 196-197

Pages 198-199

Pages 200-201

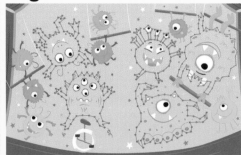

Pages 202-203

Pages 204-205

Pages 206-207

Pages 208-209

Pages 210-211

Pages 212-213

Pages 214-215

Pages 216-217

Pages 218-219

Pages 220-221

Pages 222-223

Pages 224-225

Pages 226-227

Pages 228-229

Pages 230-231

Pages 232-233

Pages 234-235

Pages 236-237

Pages 238-239

Pages 240-241

Pages 242-243

Pages 244-245

Pages 246-247

Pages 248-249

Pages 250-251